"Warrior Wisdom: The Ultimate Steph Curry Trivia Challenge"

By Jimmy Skirrts

Disclaimer

This book, "Warrior Wisdom: The Ultimate Steph Curry Trivia Challenge", is a work of independent research and compilation. The trivia questions and answers herein are based on publicly available information and are intended for entertainment and informational purposes only.

While every effort has been made to ensure the accuracy and completeness of the trivia, there may be occasional discrepancies or unintentional omissions. The author and publisher have strived to be as accurate as possible in the creation of this book but make no representations or warranties of any kind, express or implied, about the completeness, accuracy, reliability, suitability, or availability with respect to the book's content.

Furthermore, this work is not affiliated with, endorsed by, or in any way associated with Stephen Curry, the Golden State Warriors, the NBA, or any of their affiliates or representatives. All trademarks, service marks, and copyrights mentioned in this book are the property of their respective owners and are used here for illustrative purposes.

Readers are encouraged to further research any topics or events mentioned to gain a more comprehensive understanding. Any perceived slights or errors are unintentional.

Navigating the Warrior's Path: How to Use This Book

🌟 Greetings, Trivia Trailblazer!

As you stand on the precipice of this enlightening journey through the universe of Stephen Curry trivia, it's essential to familiarize yourself with the layout of "Warrior Wisdom: The Ultimate Steph Curry Trivia Challenge."

✨ The Quest Begins: Questions

Dive deep into the heart of this tome where each chapter is adorned with a series of questions. Designed to challenge your knowledge, spark your memories, and perhaps stump even the most ardent fans, these questions are crafted to unveil the intricacies and nuances of Steph's captivating journey.

✨ The Revelations Await: Answers

True mastery lies in patience, dear reader! The urge to verify your answers might be powerful, but to heighten the essence of this challenge, all the answers reside at the very end of the book. This format ensures an uninterrupted immersion into the trivia experience. So, gather your friends for a trivia night, make it a personal challenge, or simply indulge in the joy of discovery without the temptation of quick glances to the back.

💡 Note: When in doubt or deliberation, draw inspiration from the man at the heart of our trivia: "Every time I rise up, I have confidence that I'm going to make it." —Stephen Curry

🌟 Embarking on Your Adventure...

"Warrior Wisdom" is not just about questions and answers. It's an odyssey, a celebration, and an exploration of the legacy of a basketball luminary. As you traverse through its pages, savor the journey, relish the revelations, and above all, revel in the game of knowledge!

Ready yourself, trivia aficionado. May the wisdom of the Warrior guide your path!

Please note that the book is set-up to have a series of questions and then the answers will follow. Some of the questions will be repetitive to test your memory.

In the realm of sports, legends are made, not born. Their sagas are etched not just in the record books, but in the very heartbeats of their fans. And in the ever-thrilling world of basketball, Stephen Wardell Curry, the prodigy of the Golden State Warriors, has crafted his own mesmerizing tale—one that transcends the boundaries of the court and resonates deeply with millions across the globe.

"Warrior Wisdom: The Ultimate Steph Curry Trivia Challenge" is not just an homage to Curry's greatness, but an invitation to dive deeper, to seek out the intricate details of his journey, and to test the boundaries of what you think you know about the man often simply referred to as 'Steph'.

From the echoing gyms of Davidson College, where a young, unassuming guard began to show flickers of his future brilliance, to the roaring Oracle Arena and then the Chase Center, where his name would be chanted by thousands, Stephen Curry's journey is a testament to perseverance, innovation, and an unyielding belief in oneself. It's this journey that we will explore, uncovering the lesser-known tales, the behind-the-scenes anecdotes, and the surprising trivia that define his life and career.

But why Steph Curry? In a league brimming with titans, what makes this 6'2" guard from Akron, Ohio, stand out? Is it his unparalleled shooting prowess, making three-pointers look as easy as layups? Or is it his leadership, the intangible quality that rallies a team and turns them into champions? Or perhaps it's the sheer joy with which he plays, that child-like enthusiasm that's infectious to fans and players alike? Through the pages of this book, you'll discover that it's all of this and so much more.

While the accolades and records are a testament to his skill, it's the moments that aren't captured by the stat sheet that truly define him. It's the late-night practice sessions, the unwavering faith in the face of criticism, the commitment to family, and the philanthropic ventures that unveil the character of the man.

"Warrior Wisdom" is, at its core, a celebration. A celebration of a player who has defied conventions, redefined a position, and, in many ways, changed the game of basketball itself. It's also a challenge—a challenge to dive deep into the reservoir of Steph trivia, to test your knowledge, and to come out with a newfound appreciation for #30.

As you flip through these pages, you'll encounter questions that might stump you, facts that might surprise you, and stories that will undoubtedly inspire you. Whether you're a die-hard Warriors fan, an NBA enthusiast, or simply a lover of sports tales, there's something in here for everyone.

So, let the challenge begin! Immerse yourself in the world of Stephen Curry, and discover the wisdom of a Warrior.

1. Which team did Curry score 0 points against in his freshman year at Davidson leading to a notable self-motivation story?

2. Who was Curry's primary backcourt mate during his time at Davidson?

3. In the 2021 season Curry and which other player became the first set of opposing players to each score 50+ points in a game?

4. Which former NBA star is Stephen Curry's godfather?

5. How many games did it take for Curry to hit his first 1000 NBA three-pointers setting a record for the fastest to do so?

6. Who was Curry's coach when he won his first NBA championship?

7. In his third NBA game Curry recorded a then career-high in points against which team?

8. How tall is Stephen Curry?

9. Which movie did Curry mention as his favorite in multiple interviews?

10. How old was Curry when he first won the NBA MVP award?

11. Which of the following brands has Curry not collaborated with: Under Armour Nike or Palm?

12. What is the subtitle of Stephen Curry's documentary "Underrated"?

13. What title does Curry's sister Sydel hold in relation to Elon University's volleyball team?

14. How many three-pointers did Curry make in his first-ever NBA game?

15. Which NBA team did Curry score 54 points against at Madison Square Garden in 2013?

16. How many MVP awards had Stephen Curry won by the end of 2021?

17. What nickname has been commonly used to describe the tandem of Stephen Curry and Klay Thompson?

18. Curry and his wife Ayesha launched a mobile game in 2016 named what?

19. What unique feature was notable about the release of Curry's "Curry 6" shoes with Under Armour in 2019?

20. What accolade did Curry win in the 2011 NBA All-Star Weekend?

21. Curry's younger brother Seth Curry made his NBA debut with which team?

22. Curry has a pre-game ritual of doing what before every game?

23. In what year did Stephen Curry first appear in the NBA All-Star game?

24. Curry starred in commercials for which major fast-food chain?

25. Curry became the Warriors' all-time leader in three-pointers made surpassing whom?

26. What is the name of Stephen Curry's wife?

27. Against which team did Curry and the Warriors lose after leading 3-1 in the NBA Finals?

28. In which year was Stephen Curry born?

29. What is the name of Curry's charitable foundation aimed at ending child hunger?

30. Who was Curry's college coach at Davidson?

31. Which NBA Hall of Famer once said Curry was "hurting the game" because of his influence on young players?

32. Which team did Curry face in his first NBA playoff series?

33. Curry made how many three-pointers during the 2012-2013 season breaking Ray Allen's previous single-season record?

34. Which position does Stephen Curry primarily play?

35. In 2017 Curry signed a supermax contract with the Warriors worth how much over five years?

36. Curry achieved the NBA's first-ever unanimous MVP in which season?

37. Which player did Curry finish runner-up to for the 2015-2016 NBA Most Improved Player award?

38. Which brand of car featured Stephen Curry in their commercials?

39. Who did Curry face in the final round of the 2015 NBA Three-Point Contest?

40. How many points did Curry score in his first NBA game?

41. In the 2014-2015 season Curry broke his own record by making how many three-pointers?

42. From which high school did Curry graduate?

43. Curry set the NCAA season record for three-pointers made during which year of college?

44. Stephen Curry starred in a 2019 Facebook series titled what?

45. Which player's record did Curry break for the most three-pointers made in a single NBA Finals game in 2019?

46. Who was the head coach of Davidson during Curry's tenure there?

47. In which year did Curry launch the Underrated Tour aimed at highlighting overlooked high school athletes?

48. Which NBA team first drafted Stephen Curry?

49. How many games did the Golden State Warriors win in the 2014-2015 regular season marking their first championship run with Curry?

50. What is Stephen Curry's middle name?

51. Which NBA team did Curry's father Dell conclude his playing career with?

52. What is Stephen Curry's full name?

53. Which musical artist wrote a song titled "0 to 100" mentioning Curry's shooting skills?

54. What accolade did Curry receive at the 2015 ESPY Awards?

55. During the 2015-2016 NBA season which team handed the Warriors their first loss after a historic 24-0 start?

56. Stephen and Ayesha Curry have how many children?

57. Curry frequently mentions which childhood coach for instilling his shooting form?

58. Against which team did Curry make his NBA debut?

59. Who was the main sponsor for Curry's 2019 "Underrated Tour" aimed at high school players?

60. Which musical artist shouted out Curry in the song "Blessings"?

61. Curry was not heavily recruited out of high school. Which major conference school offered him a spot as a walk-on?

62. In which season did Curry lead the league in steals per game?

63. What habit does Curry frequently display while on the basketball court?

64. Which brand of water did Curry become an investor in?

65. How many rebounds per game did Curry average during the 2015-2016 NBA season?

66. In which round of the 2009 NBA Draft was Curry selected?

67. Against which team did Curry set his playoff career-high in assists during the 2019 NBA playoffs?

68. Who coached Curry during the 2014 FIBA Basketball World Cup?

69. What nickname is given to the duo of Stephen Curry and Klay Thompson?

70. Which former U.S. President played golf with Stephen Curry in 2015?

71. In 2016 Curry broke his own NBA record for fastest player to make how many three-pointers in a season?

72. Which of Curry's children shares his birthday month of March?

73. Against which team did Curry score his career-high 62 points in January 2021?

74. Which PGA Tour event did Curry participate in during 2017 and 2018?

75. In 2013 Curry set a then-NBA season record for three-pointers made. How many did he make?

76. Which overseas brand did Curry sign a shoe deal with in 2013?

77. At what age did Curry first beat his father Dell in a game of one-on-one?

78. What is the name of Curry's son?

79. In 2013 Curry and which other player set the NBA record for most combined three-pointers by teammates in a season?

80. Which sibling of Stephen Curry also plays in the NBA?

81. Who was the primary defender against Curry during the 2016 NBA Finals from the Cleveland Cavaliers?

82. What is the name of Stephen Curry's autobiography?

83. Curry and which other player were the only unanimous MVPs in NBA history by the end of 2021?

84. In which year was Curry's younger brother Seth born?

85. Which player's behind-the-back move did Curry emulate in the 2019 NBA All-Star Game to make a three-pointer?

86. What number does Stephen Curry wear for the Golden State Warriors?

87. What's the name of the NBA shooting competition that Curry won during the 2015 All-Star weekend?

88. What accolade did Curry win during the 2011 NBA All-Star Weekend?

89. In his NBA career Curry hit 10+ three-pointers in a game multiple times. Against which team did he first accomplish this feat?

90. Stephen Curry has a tattoo in Hebrew that translates to what?

91. Stephen Curry once missed how many three-pointers in a single playoff game setting an unfortunate record?

92. Who did Curry and the Warriors defeat in the 2015 NBA Finals?

93. Which shoe model by Under Armour was widely mocked on social media and dubbed the "Chef Curry"?

94. Against which team did Curry have his first-ever NBA triple-double?

95. How many regular-season games did the Warriors win during Curry's rookie season?

96. Which wrist did Curry fracture during the 2019-2020 season?

97. Curry wore the number 20 during which international basketball competition?

98. Which ankle did Curry repeatedly injure early in his career?

99. In which year did Curry first average more than 20 points per game in the NBA?

100. Which team did Curry face when he made his NBA postseason debut?

101. What distinctive feature is present on the court at the Oracle Arena (Warriors' previous home) that is associated with Curry?

102. In the 2017 NBA Finals how many points did Curry average per game?

103. In which season did Curry become the fastest player to hit 100 three-pointers?

104. How many points did Curry score in his NBA debut?

105. Which retired NBA player known for his three-point shooting said Curry and Klay Thompson might be the best shooting backcourt in NBA history?

106. What's the name of Curry's first signature shoe with Under Armour?

107. In 2018 Curry produced a documentary about which church's tragic event?

108. In which season did Curry become a part of the NBA's 50-40-90 club?

109. Which former NBA player is known for mentoring and training Curry during his early NBA career?

110. In Curry's 2017 animated series what's the name of the lead character he voices?

111. In 2013 Curry and his wife Ayesha launched a non-profit organization with what name?

112. Which team did Curry drop his then career-high 44 points against in 2010?

113. In which year did Curry surpass Ray Allen's record for the most three-pointers in a postseason?

114. In 2019 Curry and Ayesha Curry launched a scholarship program for which university?

115. Which shoe model released by Under Armour was infamously nicknamed the "Dad Shoes"?

116. Which NBA player known for his defensive prowess claimed in an interview that guarding Curry was harder than guarding LeBron James?

117. In which year did Curry win his first NBA Championship with the Warriors?

118. Stephen Curry and which other NBA player jointly received the NBA Community Assist Award in 2014?

119. What special recognition did Curry's Davidson team receive despite not winning the NCAA championship?

120. How many points did Curry score in the 3rd quarter against the New Orleans Pelicans in 2015 tying the NBA record for points in a quarter?

121. Which player did Curry surpass in January 2019 to move into third place for all-time NBA three-pointers made?

122. Which NBA player playfully mocked Curry's shimmy dance after hitting a three-pointer against the Warriors in 2018?

123. What childhood game did Curry and his brother Seth play to improve their shooting skills?

124. Who did the Golden State Warriors trade to clear the way for Curry to be their starting point guard during his rookie season?

125. What was unique about the design of Curry's signature Under Armour shoes released for International Women's Day in 2019?

126. Against which team did Curry make his famous 37-foot game-winning shot in 2016?

127. During which season did Curry surpass his father Dell in career NBA points?

128. What is the significance of the "I can do all things..." phrase for Curry?

129. Curry set an NBA record for most consecutive games with a made three-pointer. How many games was this streak?

130. Who did the Golden State Warriors draft in 2009 immediately after selecting Stephen Curry?

131. Which player was chosen right before Stephen Curry in the 2009 NBA Draft?

132. Curry's daughter Riley became an internet sensation after appearing in a post-game press conference during which year's NBA playoffs?

133. Curry's 77 consecutive made three-pointers in practice was witnessed by which teammate?

134. Which NBA Hall of Famer mentioned in an interview that he believed his prime version would "kill" Stephen Curry one-on-one?

135. Who was the head coach of the Golden State Warriors when Curry was drafted?

136. Curry has frequently spoken about his faith. Which Bible verse is he known to write on his sneakers?

137. Curry once famously remarked "I'm back!" during a playoff game against which team?

138. Curry has been involved in various charity golf events. Which other NBA legend often joins him?

139. Curry's shoe deal with Nike ended in which year before he switched to Under Armour?

140. During which season did Stephen Curry break his own single-season record by making 402 three-pointers?

141. During his college career at Davidson Curry led the Wildcats to the NCAA Tournament how many times?

142. In which year did Curry lead Davidson to the Elite Eight of the NCAA Tournament?

143. Who was the starting center for the Golden State Warriors during Curry's MVP seasons in 2015 and 2016?

144. How many points did Curry score in his highest-scoring game during his college career at Davidson?

145. Which video game series featured Curry as its cover athlete in 2015 and 2016?

146. Which player alongside Curry started in the Warriors' backcourt during their 2015 NBA championship season?

147. Which childhood friend and NBA player did Curry face in the 2019 NBA Finals?

148. During the 2015 NBA Finals Curry made a behind-the-head pass to which teammate for a dunk?

149. In which year did Curry and the Warriors first face the Houston Rockets in the NBA playoffs?

150. In 2016 Curry became the first player in NBA history to be voted MVP by how many votes?

151. Which team did the Warriors defeat in Curry's first Western Conference Finals appearance?

152. In which season did Curry lead the league in free throw percentage for the first time?

153. Which former NBA player known for his defense claimed he could shut down Curry in his prime?

154. Which NBA team did Stephen's brother Seth Curry play for in the 2021 season?

155. How many three-pointers did Curry make in the 2015-16 season setting a new NBA record?

156. What is the colorway name of the Curry One shoes that were released in honor of the Warriors' 2015 championship?

157. Curry made a guest appearance on which popular HBO TV series in 2019?

158. What company did Curry co-found which focuses on media branding and investments?

159. Which fellow NBA superstar joined the Golden State Warriors in 2016 forming a dynamic duo with Curry?

160. In the 2017 NBA playoffs against which team did Curry have a dance celebration after making a layup?

161. In which NBA city did Curry grow up attending games because of his father's career?

162. In a game against the Washington Wizards in 2016 how many three-pointers did Curry make to tie the NBA single-game record?

163. Who was the opponent when Curry surpassed Wilt Chamberlain to become the Warriors' all-time leading scorer in 2021?

164. Which NBA player was involved in a notable shimmy dance "battle" with Curry during the 2018 Western Conference Finals?

165. In which city was the Under Armour store located where Curry surprised a group of high school athletes by joining their tour?

166. Stephen Curry's mothernSonya Curry played collegiate volleyball for which university?

167. Which other NBA player from the 2009 draft class has played with Curry on the Warriors?

168. Against which team did Curry achieve his career-high in steals during a game in 2016?

169. How many three-pointers did Curry make in a single game against the Memphis Grizzlies in 2017 to set a then Warriors' record?

170. In what year did Curry and the Warriors achieve a record 73 regular-season wins?

171. By the end of 2021 how many NBA All-Star games had Curry participated in?

172. Which animated movie franchise featured Stephen Curry voicing a character in its 2018 installment?

173. Curry's daughter Riley gained widespread attention for her appearances during which event?

174. In the early years of his NBA career Curry battled injuries primarily in which part of his body?

175. Which team did the Warriors play against in Curry's first-ever Christmas Day game in the NBA?

176. Curry appeared in a series of commercials mocking "basketball lessons" with which other NBA player?

177. In which NBA All-Star Game did Curry finish with a double-double of points and rebounds?

178. What's the name of the kid-friendly show Curry appeared on to promote healthy habits?

179. In the 2019 playoffs against which team did Curry score 33 points in the second half of a game?

1. Michigan.

2. Jason Richards.

3. Kevin Durant.

4. Greg Bracey.

5. 369 Games.

6. Steve Kerr.

7. Phoenix Suns.

8. 6 Feet 2 Inches.

9. A Few Good Men.

10. 27.

11. Nike.

12. "Against All Odds".

13. All-time Assists Leader.

14. 0.

15. New York Knicks.

16. 2.

17. Splash Brothers.

18. Chef Curry.

19. It Had A Sock-like Design.

20. Skills Challenge.

21. Sacramento Kings.

22. Taking A Shot From The Tunnel.

23. 2014.

24. Burger King.

25. Jason Richardson.

26. Ayesha Curry.

27. Cleveland Cavaliers.

28. 1988.

29. Eat. Learn. Play.

30. Bob McKillop.

31. Oscar Robertson.

32. Denver Nuggets.

33. 272.

34. Point Guard.

35. $201 Million.

36. 2015-2016.

37. C.J. McCollum.

38. Infiniti.

39. Klay Thompson.

40. 14.

41. 286.

42. Charlotte Christian.

43. Sophomore.

44. Stephen Vs The Game.

45. Ray Allen.

46. Bob McKillop.

47. 2019.

48. Golden State Warriors.

49. 67.

50. Ward.

51. Toronto Raptors.

52. Wardell Stephen Curry II.

53. Drake.

54. Best Male Athlete.

55. Milwaukee Bucks.

56. Three.

57. Dell Curry (his Father).

58. Houston Rockets.

59. Under Armour.

60. Big Sean.

61. Virginia Tech.

62. 2015-2016.

63. Chewing On His Mouthguard.

64. Brita.

65. 5.4.

66. First Round.

67. Los Angeles Clippers.

68. Mike Krzyzewski.

69. Splash Brothers.

70. Barack Obama.

71. 300.

72. Riley.

73. Portland Trail Blazers.

74. Ellie Mae Classic.

75. 272.

76. Under Armour.

77. 14.

78. Canon.

79. Klay Thompson.

80. Seth Curry.

81. Kyrie Irving.

82. Underrated.

83. Giannis Antetokounmpo.

84. 1990.

85. Dirk Nowitzki.

86. 30.

87. Three-Point Contest.

88. Taco Bell Skills Challenge.

89. Denver Nuggets.

90. "Love Never Fails."

91. 13.

92. Cleveland Cavaliers.

93. Curry 2 Low "Chef".

94. Los Angeles Clippers.

95. 26.

96. Left Wrist.

97. 2010 FIBA World Championship.

98. Right Ankle.

99. 2012-2013.

100. Denver Nuggets.

101. A Caricature Of His "celebration Shimmy".

102. 26.8.

103. 2016-2017.

104. 14.

105. Reggie Miller.

106. Curry One.

107. Emanuel African Methodist Episcopal Church In Charleston.

108. 2015-2016.

109. Steve Nash.

110. Cordell.

111. Eat. Learn. Play.

112. New York Knicks.

113. 2015.

114. University Of Tokyo.

115. Curry 2 Low "Chef".

116. Tony Allen.

117. 2015.

118. Dwyane Wade.

119. Their Jersey Was Retired At The Davidson Arena.

120. 28.

121. Jason Terry.

122. LeBron James.

123. P-I-G.

124. Monta Ellis.

125. Designed By A 9-year-old Girl.

126. Oklahoma City Thunder.

127. 2013-2014.

128. It's His Motto And He Writes It On His Shoes Before Every Game.

129. 157.

130. They Didn't Draft Anyone Else In The First Round After Curry In 2009.

131. Hasheem Thabeet.

132. 2015.

133. Draymond Green.

134. Michael Jordan.

135. Don Nelson.

136. Philippians 4:13.

137. Portland Trail Blazers.

138. Chris Paul.

139. 2013.

140. 2015-2016.

141. Three.

142. 2008.

143. Andrew Bogut.

144. 44.

145. NBA 2K.

146. Klay Thompson.

147. Fred VanVleet.

148. Andre Iguodala.

149. 2015.

150. Unanimously.

151. Houston Rockets.

152. 2010-2011.

153. Gary Payton.

154. Philadelphia 76ers.

155. 402.

156. "Champ Pack".

157. Ballers.

158. SC30 Inc.

159. Kevin Durant.

160. Cleveland Cavaliers.

161. Charlotte.

162. 11.

163. Denver Nuggets.

164. Chris Paul.

165. Shanghai.

166. Virginia Tech.

167. Draymond Green.

168. Atlanta Hawks.

169. 13.

170. 2016.

171. 7.

172. "Penguins Of Madagascar".

173. Post-game Press Conferences.

174. Ankles.

175. Cleveland Cavaliers.

176. Chris Paul.

177. 2019.

178. Sesame Street.

179. Houston Rockets.

1. How many points did Curry average during his final college season at Davidson?

2. Which collegiate conference did Curry play in while at Davidson?

3. What is the name of Stephen Curry's production company which he co-founded?

4. What is Stephen Curry's middle name?

5. In which year did Curry first participate in the NBA's Three-Point Contest?

6. During which season did Curry score his career-high 62 points?

7. In which year did Curry have his first double-double in an NBA All-Star game?

8. What is the name of Curry's younger sister?

9. During which playoff series did Curry famously point to the sky after making a deep three-pointer acknowledging his faith?

10. How many assists did Curry average during his rookie season?

11. In which game of the 2018 NBA Finals did Curry set the Finals record for most three-pointers in a game?

12. During the 2016-2017 season how many games did Curry play?

13. In which charity event did Curry play golf with former President Barack Obama?

14. What accolade did Curry receive during the 2014 FIBA World Cup?

15. Which NBA player during his Hall of Fame induction speech said he knew he had to retire when he couldn't guard rookie Stephen Curry?

16. Which high school did Stephen Curry attend?

17. Which player did Curry pass in December 2020 to become second on the all-time three-pointers list?

18. How many games did Curry play in the 2017 NBA Finals?

19. What honor did Curry receive from the Associated Press in December 2015?

20. How many children does Stephen Curry have as of 2021?

21. What is the name of Stephen Curry's basketball-playing maternal grandfather?

22. In which All-Star Game did Curry win the Three-Point Contest?

23. How many rebounds per game did Stephen Curry average during his unanimous MVP season?

24. How many assists did Curry average during the 2018-2019 NBA season?

25. Which fellow NBA player is a frequent golfing buddy of Stephen Curry's?

26. Who was Curry's teammate and fellow "Splash Brother" at Davidson?

27. What is the record for the longest streak of games with at least one three-pointer made by Curry?

28. How many points did Curry average during the 2018 NBA Playoffs?

29. How many points per game did Curry average during his sophomore year of college?

30. How many turnovers did Curry have in Game 7 of the 2016 NBA Finals?

31. Which NBA team did Curry play against in his first ever NBA playoff game?

32. Curry's mother Sonya Curry played which sport in college?

33. How many steals per game did Curry average in his MVP season of 2015-2016?

34. In which NBA All-Star game did Curry finish with 11 assists?

35. Which former NBA star said that Curry "has changed the whole geometry of the game?"

36. Against which team did Curry have his first NBA triple-double?

37. How many steals did Curry record in his record-breaking 2015-2016 MVP season?

38. For how many seasons did Curry play college basketball at Davidson?

39. In which year did Curry and the Warriors set the regular-season record with 73 wins?

40. How many points did Curry score in his NBA debut?

41. What injury kept Curry out of many games during the beginning of his NBA career?

42. Against which team did Curry break this record?

43. How many times had Curry been ejected from an NBA game as of the end of the 2020-2021 season?

44. How many points did Curry score in his debut game at Davidson?

45. What is the title of the movie in which Curry appeared in 2015 alongside LeBron James?

46. What's the name of Stephen Curry's oldest daughter?

47. In a humorous moment which fellow NBA star tried (and failed) to mimic Curry's tunnel shot routine before a game?

48. Who was Curry's first head coach in the NBA?

49. Which NBA player known for his dunks said that Curry is "changing the game"?

50. Who coached Stephen Curry during his time at Davidson College?

51. How many times has Curry been selected to the NBA All-Defensive Team?

52. How many regular-season MVP awards has Stephen Curry won as of 2021?

53. How many technical fouls did Curry receive during the 2019-2020 season?

54. In which round of the 2009 NBA Draft was Stephen Curry selected?

55. Which documentary released in 2018 followed Stephen Curry's off-the-court experiences including his overseas tours?

56. How tall is Stephen Curry?

57. Which NBA player after being asked about Curry's defensive abilities famously said "He can't guard me" during a post-game interview?

58. In the 2015 NBA Finals how many points did Curry average?

59. In Curry's first ever NBA game which team did the Warriors play against?

60. Which shoe size does Stephen Curry wear?

61. Who was the head coach of the Warriors when Curry made his first All-Star appearance?

62. Who was the primary defender on Curry during the 2015 NBA Finals?

63. Which team did Stephen Curry play against in his first Christmas Day NBA game?

64. In which game of the 2015 NBA Finals did Curry score 37 points?

65. In which year did Curry launch his Underrated Tour a basketball camp for underrated high school athletes?

66. How many three-pointers did Curry make during his rookie season?

67. Who was Curry's backup point guard during the 2015 NBA championship run?

68. How many siblings does Stephen Curry have?

69. Which team did Curry make the game-winning three-point shot against with 0.6 seconds left in overtime in December 2015?

70. In what year did Stephen Curry win the NBA Sportsmanship Award?

71. Which two players joined Curry in the Warriors' "Death Lineup" during the 2014-2015 season?

72. In 2018 Curry was involved in a multi-car crash in which city?

73. How many three-pointers did Curry make in the 2016 NBA All-Star game?

74. Against which team did Curry score 51 points in October 2018?

75. Stephen Curry has appeared on which late-night talk show multiple times?

76. In which year was Curry's jersey the best-selling in the NBA?

77. In which year did Curry first achieve a triple-double in an NBA game?

78. How many free throws did Curry attempt in the 2017 NBA Finals?

79. Which player did Curry notably cross over before hitting a three in a game against the Clippers in 2015?

80. In which season did Curry first lead the league in scoring?

81. Which team did the Warriors face in Curry's first ever NBA playoff series?

82. What's the name of Stephen Curry's wife?

83. Against which team did Curry make his return from a hand injury in March 2020?

84. Which team drafted Curry's father Dell Curry?

85. During which NBA All-Star game did Curry complete a bounce alley-oop pass to Giannis Antetokounmpo?

86. In which year did Curry win the ESPY Award for Best Male Athlete?

87. In his unanimous MVP season Curry made a record for consecutive games with a three-pointer. How many games was this streak?

88. What was Curry's field goal percentage during the 2014-2015 season?

89. Which NBA legend did Curry overtake in postseason three-pointers during the 2015 playoffs?

90. In the 2017-2018 season how many games did Curry miss due to injury?

91. Curry's brother Seth Curry plays in the NBA as well. Which team was he playing for during the 2020-2021 season?

92. During which playoff series did Curry famously shimmy after making a three-point shot against the Pelicans' defense?

93. Which two teams did the Warriors face in the Western Conference Finals in 2016 and 2017 respectively?

94. How many points did Curry score in his highest-scoring game at Davidson?

95. Against which Eastern Conference team did Curry score 54 points in 2013?

96. Which famed NBA coach described Curry's game style as "changing the way the game is played" in a positive manner?

97. Curry's father Dell Curry played the majority of his NBA career with which team?

98. In which season did Curry lead the league in free throw percentage for the first time?

99. What is the name of Stephen Curry's first signature shoe with Under Armour?

100. Which brand did Stephen Curry collaborate with for his "Curry Brand" of clothing and shoes?

101. How many turnovers per game did Curry average in his unanimous MVP season?

102. How many assists did Curry average during his unanimous MVP season in 2015-2016?

103. In the 2019 NBA Finals Curry set a new record for the most consecutive free throws made. How many did he make?

104. How many three-pointers did Curry make in the 2015 NBA All-Star game?

105. Which former NBA player also known for his shooting mentored Curry during his early NBA years?

106. Which team did the Warriors face in their first NBA Finals appearance during Curry's tenure in 2015?

107. Which player was the other guard starting alongside Curry in his rookie season?

108. During his college years which team did Davidson upset in the NCAA tournament making Curry a household name?

109. How many games did the Golden State Warriors lose in their 73-win season?

110. In which season did Curry become the Warriors' all-time leader in three-point field goals?

111. Who served as the Warriors' interim head coach during Steve Kerr's medical absence leading the team alongside Curry?

112. What was Stephen Curry's free throw percentage during the 2015-2016 season?

113. Which NBA legend said that Curry and Nash had "changed the perception of what a point guard is"?

114. During which year's playoffs did Curry have a memorable game where he declared "I'm back!" after returning from an injury?

115. In a game against which team did Curry make a then-record 13 three-pointers in 2016?

116. In 2019 against which team did Curry make a layup with 0.5 seconds left to send the game to overtime?

117. Which other NBA sharpshooter shares the same birthday with Stephen Curry?

118. Curry and Klay Thompson combined hold the record for the most number of three-pointers by a duo in a season. How many did they make in 2014-2015?

119. How many offensive rebounds did Curry average during the 2017-2018 NBA season?

120. Against which former NBA MVP did Curry famously use a

behind-the-back dribble before hitting a step-back three during the 2016 playoffs?

121. In the 2014-2015 season the Warriors started with a record streak. How many games did they win consecutively to start the season?

122. Against which team did Curry hit a buzzer-beating game-winner in the 2014-2015 season after dribbling through multiple defenders?

123. Which player was guarding Curry when he hit the game-winner with 2.1 seconds left against the Mavericks in 2014?

124. Which Hall of Famer said "Steph Curry is the best shooter I've ever seen?"?

125. In which year did Curry and the Warriors visit the White House to celebrate their NBA championship?

126. Against which team did Curry make a half-court shot right before halftime in the 2016 playoffs?

127. How many three-pointers did Curry make in the 2019 NBA All-Star game?

128. Which player did Curry cross over before hitting a three-pointer leading to memes about the player's ankles?

129. Which former NBA player known for his defense took Curry under his wing during his rookie season with the Warriors?

130. In which season did Curry surpass Ray Allen's single-season three-pointer record for the first time?

131. Which team did the Warriors beat in Curry's first NBA Finals victory?

132. Who held the record for most three-pointers made in a season before Stephen Curry broke it?

133. Which NBA legend said that Curry is "the best thing since sliced bread?"

134. What number does Stephen Curry wear on his Golden State Warriors jersey?

135. Who was Golden State's general manager when Stephen Curry was drafted in 2009?

136. How many three-pointers did Curry make in the 2015 NBA All-Star game?

137. In 2015 Curry made an appearance in a comedy movie alongside which other NBA superstar?

138. How many times did Curry score 40 or more points in a game during the 2016-2017 regular season?

139. In which city did Curry host the "Stephen Curry Select Camp" for top high school point guards?

140. Against which team did Curry have his first 50-point game in the NBA?

141. Against which team did Curry sink a game-winning three-pointer from almost half-court in 2016?

142. Which NBA team did Curry's father Dell Curry play for when Stephen was born?

143. Which musician has frequently been seen at Warriors games and even wore a Curry jersey during one of his concerts?

144. Which team did the Warriors beat in the 2017 Western Conference Finals?

145. Who was the Golden State Warriors head coach before Steve Kerr took over in 2014?

146. What is the name of the YouTube series that documented Stephen Curry's 2018 summer and preparation for the next season?

147. In the 2019-2020 season Curry only played a few games due to injury. How many games did he play that season?

148. Against which team did Curry have a memorable shimmy after hitting a three in the 2018 Western Conference Finals?

149. What was the primary color of the "Chef Curry" shoes that became a social media sensation?

150. Who was the Warriors' leading scorer in the game where Curry hit the half-court shot to beat the Thunder in 2016?

151. Which coach said that Curry "was ruining the game" in jest referencing how kids were trying to emulate his playing style?

152. Who did Stephen Curry replace in the starting lineup during his rookie season with the Warriors?

153. Which player did Stephen Curry bring along to the 2018 NBA All-Star draft to ensure they were on the same team?

154. Which retired NBA player known for his commentary once said "Steph Curry is not a point guard or a shooting guard. He's a hybrid."?

155. Against which team did Curry achieve his highest-scoring playoff game?

156. Who did Stephen Curry credit for teaching him the floater shot which became a staple of his game?

157. During the infamous 2016 Game 7 of the NBA Finals how many points did Curry score?

158. Against which team did Curry make a playoff career-high nine three-pointers in 2018?

159. Which NBA player jokingly said that Curry's game-winning three against Oklahoma City in 2016 "wasn't a good shot"?

160. In a viral moment from the 2019 NBA Finals which rapper did Curry share a conversation with on the sidelines?

161. Who was Golden State's primary center during their 2017 and 2018 championship runs?

162. What was Curry's three-point shooting percentage during his senior year at Davidson?

163. Which coach was in charge of the Golden State Warriors when they drafted Stephen Curry?

164. Which NBA player known for his defense said guarding Curry was "challenging" and "fun"?

165. Which fellow NBA superstar joined the Warriors in the summer of 2016 creating a 'super team'?

166. Against which team did Curry have a double-double in his first NBA playoff game?

167. Which rapper mentioned Stephen Curry in his song "0 to 100/The Catch Up"?

168. Curry once hit a game-winner against which NBA team on "Chinese New Year" night?

169. Which childhood friend and NBA player often worked out with Curry during the summers?

170. During his unanimous MVP season how many times did Curry score 50 or more points in a game?

171. Which of Curry's college games is most remembered for his leading Davidson with 33 points to upset a 2-seed team in the NCAA tournament?

172. What record did Curry set in his second game of the 2016 NBA Finals in terms of three-pointers made?

173. Which basketball legend referred to Curry as "the greatest shooter I've ever seen?"

174. Against which team did Curry score 54 points in Madison Square Garden in 2013?

175. What was the Golden State Warriors' record during the 2017-2018 regular season with Curry in the lineup?

176. During a game in early 2021 Curry made headlines by scoring how

many points?

177. How many minutes per game did Curry average during his rookie season?

178. In the 2019 NBA Finals against which team did the Golden State Warriors compete?

179. Before breaking his own record how many three-pointers did Curry make in the 2014-2015 season to set a new NBA record?

180. Who was the main rival of the Golden State Warriors during Curry's multiple NBA Finals appearances?

181. In which year did Stephen Curry appear in the NBA Celebrity All-Star Game as a coach?

182. Which video game featured Stephen Curry James Harden and Anthony Davis on its covers in 2015?

183. Who is the author of the biography "Rise and Shine: The Extraordinary Story of Stephen Curry"?

1. 28.6.

2. Southern Conference.

3. Unanimous Media.

4. Wardell.

5. 2010.

6. 2020-2021.

7. 2017.

8. Sydel Curry.

9. 2013 NBA Playoffs Against Denver Nuggets.

10. 5.9.

11. Game 2.

12. 79.

13. The Ellie Mae Classic.

14. Tournament MVP.

15. Jason Kidd.

16. Charlotte Christian.

17. Reggie Miller.

18. 5.

19. Male Athlete Of The Year.

20. 3.

21. Jack "Jumpshot" Vaughn.

22. 2015.

23. 5.4.

24. 5.2.

25. Andre Iguodala.

26. There Wasn't A "Splash Brother" At Davidson The Term Is Reserved For His Partne

27. 157 Games.

28. 25.5.

29. 25.9.

30. 4.

31. Denver Nuggets.

32. Volleyball.

33. 21.

34. 2017.

35. Steve Nash.

36. Los Angeles Clippers.

37. 169.

38. 3 Seasons.

39. 2016.

40. 14.

41. Ankle Injuries.

42. New Orleans Pelicans.

43. 2.

44. 15.

45. "Trainwreck".

46. Riley Curry.

47. LeBron James.

48. Don Nelson.

49. Vince Carter.

50. Bob McKillop.

51. He Hasn't Been Selected To The NBA All-Defensive Team.

52. 2.

53. 1.

54. 1st Round.

55. "Stephen Vs The Game".

56. 6 Feet 2 Inches.

57. James Harden.

58. 26.

59. Houston Rockets.

60. 13.5.

61. Mark Jackson.

62. Matthew Dellavedova.

63. Cleveland Cavaliers.

64. Game 5.

65. 2019.

66. 166.

67. Shaun Livingston.

68. 2 (Seth Curry And Sydel Curry).

69. Oklahoma City Thunder.

70. 2011.

71. Draymond Green And Klay Thompson.

72. Oakland.

73. 6.

74. Washington Wizards.

75. "The Late Show With Stephen Colbert".

76. 2016.

77. 2010.

78. 45.

79. Chris Paul.

80. 2015-2016.

81. Denver Nuggets.

82. Ayesha Curry.

83. Toronto Raptors.

84. Utah Jazz.

85. 2019.

86. 2015.

87. 152.

88. 48.7 .

89. Reggie Miller.

90. 31.

91. Philadelphia 76ers.

92. 2018 Western Conference Semifinals.

93. Oklahoma City Thunder And San Antonio Spurs.

94. 44.

95. New York Knicks.

96. Gregg Popovich.

97. Charlotte Hornets.

98. 2010-2011.

99. Curry One.

100. Under Armour.

101. 3.3.

102. 6.7.

103. 47.

104. 13.

105.   Steve Nash.

106.   Cleveland Cavaliers.

107.   Monta Ellis.

108.   Georgetown.

109.   9.

110.   2014-2015.

111.   Luke Walton.

112.   90.8 .

113. Magic Johnson.

114. 2016.

115. New Orleans Pelicans.

116. Sacramento Kings.

117. Trae Young.

118. 525.

119. 0.7.

120. Russell Westbrook.

129. Ronny Turiaf.

130. 2012-2013.

131. Cleveland Cavaliers.

132. Ray Allen.

133. Magic Johnson.

134. 30.

135. Larry Riley.

136. 5.

137. LeBron James.

138. 10.

139. Walnut Creek California.

140. New York Knicks.

141. Oklahoma City Thunder.

142. Cleveland Cavaliers.

143. Drake.

144. San Antonio Spurs.

145. Mark Jackson.

146. "5 Minutes From Home".

147. 5.

148. Houston Rockets.

149. White.

150. Kevin Durant Wasn't On The Team Then So The Leading Scorer Was Stephen Curry Hi

151. Steve Kerr.

152. Monta Ellis.

153. Klay Thompson.

154. Kenny Smith.

155. Portland Trail Blazers.

156. Steve Nash.

157. 17.

158. Cleveland Cavaliers.

159. Paul George.

160. Drake.

161. Zaza Pachulia.

162. 38.7 .

163. Don Nelson.

164. Tony Allen.

165. Kevin Durant.

166. Denver Nuggets.

167. Drake.

168. Los Angeles Clippers.

169. Chris Paul.

170. 3.

171. Against Gonzaga.

172. Most Three-pointers Made In An NBA Finals Game With 9.

173. Steve Kerr.

174. New York Knicks.

175. 41-10.

176. 62.

177. 36.2.

178. Toronto Raptors.

179. 286.

180. Cleveland Cavaliers.

181. 2018.

182. NBA 2K16.

183. Mike Yorkey.

1. Which NBA team did the Warriors face and defeat in the first round of the 2017 NBA Playoffs?

2. Who was the primary point guard Curry faced in the 2015 NBA Finals?

3. In 2014 against which team did Curry set the NBA record for most three-pointers in a month?

4. How many regular-season MVP awards has Curry won as of 2021?

5. In 2016 Curry set a new NBA record for most three-pointers made in a single game. How many did he make?

6. How many MVP awards had Curry won by the end of 2021?

7. Which sports brand did Curry initially have a sponsorship deal with before switching to Under Armour?

8. Who was Curry's teammate and fellow "Splash Brother"?

9. In which season did Curry lead the league in free throw percentage for the first time?

10. In what round of the NBA draft was Stephen Curry selected?

11. In which season did Curry lead the NBA in free throw percentage for the first time?

12. In which city did Stephen Curry grow up?

13. Which arena are the Warriors scheduled to move into for the 2019-2020 season?

14. Which team did Curry face in his first-ever NBA playoff series?

15. What is the name of the Curry family's charity that aims to provide underprivileged children with an education?

16. What injury sidelined Curry for most of the 2019-2020 season?

17. Which Western Conference team did the Warriors beat in the 2019 playoffs despite Curry shooting 0-for-9 in a half?

18. Which shoe company does Curry have an endorsement deal with?

19. Who set the record for the youngest player to score 50+ points in a game before Curry broke it in 2013?

20. In which year was Curry's jersey number retired at Davidson College?

21. Which Eastern Conference team did the Warriors face in the NBA Finals in both 2015 and 2016?

22. How many three-pointers did Curry make in his NBA debut?

23. Which NBA player described guarding Curry as "hopeless" due to his shooting ability?

24. For which NBA team does Curry's brother-in-law Damion Lee play?

25. Curry made a record for consecutive games with a three-pointer. How many games was it?

26. Curry has a tattoo in Hebrew. What does it translate to in English?

27. How many steals per game did Curry average during his unanimous MVP season in 2015-2016?

28. Which sibling of Stephen Curry also plays in the NBA?

29. In the 2017-2018 season against which team did Curry sprain his ankle leading him to miss several games?

30. What is the name of Stephen Curry's wife?

31. Which NBA team did Curry's brother Seth Curry play for during the 2018-2019 season?

32. What's the name of Stephen Curry's mother?

33. Which famous basketball coach described Curry's ball-handling as "magical"?

34. Which film company did Stephen Curry co-found?

35. Which former NBA player and analyst described Curry's shooting as "a revolution"?

36. How many points did Curry score in his NBA debut?

37. Which former NBA player and ESPN analyst called Curry and the Warriors "soft" during their 73-9 season?

38. Which teammate of Curry's won the NBA Finals MVP in 2015?

39. Against which team did Curry and the Golden State Warriors clinch their third NBA championship in four years in 2018?

40. Which fellow NBA player has a signature shoe called the "Harden"?

41. Which team did the Golden State Warriors defeat in the 2017 NBA Finals to win their second championship in three years?

42. Who coached the Warriors before Steve Kerr took over in 2014?

43. Who was the Golden State Warriors' general manager when Curry was drafted in 2009?

44. Who was Curry's coach at Davidson College?

45. Which fellow NBA player starred alongside Curry in a series of State Farm commercials as his "twin"?

46. How many games did the 2015 NBA Finals last?

47. Who was Curry's backup point guard during the 2015 NBA championship season?

48. Which number does Stephen Curry wear for the Golden State Warriors?

49. Who is the GM of the Golden State Warriors instrumental in building the team around Curry?

50. Which former U.S. president played golf with Curry in 2015?

51. Which team did the Warriors face in Curry's first NBA Finals appearance?

52. Curry played his 400th NBA game against which team?

53. Who was the general manager of the Golden State Warriors when Stephen Curry was drafted?

54. How many siblings does Curry have?

55. Against which team did Curry achieve his career-high in points scoring 62 in January 2021?

56. Which former MVP joined the Warriors for the 2016-2017 season?

57. Which player was Curry's main rival for the MVP award in the 2014-2015 season?

58. Who was the Warriors' leading scorer in Curry's rookie season?

59. Which NBA player said Curry was "just a shooter" before his MVP seasons fueling Curry's motivation?

60. In which Chinese city did Curry host a basketball camp in 2017?

61. Curry's playstyle is often credited with changing the NBA's focus to which aspect of the game?

62. Which of Curry's children was born in July 2018?

63. In which year did Curry launch his first signature shoe with Under Armour?

64. Which award did Curry win at the 2015 ESPY Awards?

65. How many points did Curry score in his first NBA Finals game in 2015?

66. How many kids do Stephen and Ayesha Curry have?

67. Which player held the record for most threes in a season before Curry broke it in 2012-2013?

68. Curry often celebrates made three-pointers with which dance move?

69. Which NBA player known for his defense claimed he loved guarding Curry because it was a challenge?

70. What's the name of Stephen Curry's wife?

71. Which team did the Warriors defeat to secure their 73rd win in the 2015-2016 season?

72. Curry wears the jersey number 30 in honor of whom?

73. Who was Curry's main defensive assignment during the 2015 NBA Finals?

74. Which college did Seth Curry play basketball for?

75. Which former NBA player and coach once jokingly said that Curry was "ruining the game" due to his deep shooting?

76. Against which team did Curry record his first career triple-double?

77. Which fellow NBA star did Curry face in the 2015 and 2019 NBA All-Star Three-Point Contests?

78. In what season did Curry lead the NBA in steals per game?

79. In which game of the 2016 NBA Finals did Curry get ejected for throwing his mouthguard?

80. How many points did Curry score in his NBA debut?

81. Curry has made several appearances on which late-night talk show hosted by James Corden?

82. How many threes did Curry make in the 2013 NBA All-Star game?

83. In 2017 who did Curry lose to in a three-point shooting contest at the NBA All-Star weekend?

84. Against which team did Curry make his NBA debut?

85. In 2016 Curry became the first unanimous MVP in NBA history. Who was the previous MVP before him to come closest to being unanimous?

86. Which of Curry's parents also played in the NBA?

87. What injury did Curry sustain in 2011 that caused him to miss significant playing time?

88. How many games did the Warriors lose in the 2017 playoffs?

89. Against which team did Curry score a double-double in his first NBA playoff game?

90. Which high school did Curry attend in Charlotte North Carolina?

91. What's the name of Stephen Curry's father who also played in the NBA?

92. In which season did Curry become the NBA's first unanimous MVP?

93. Which player did Stephen Curry credit as an influence on his floater game?

94. Against which team did Curry make his NBA debut?

95. Which international basketball player claimed to have modeled his shooting form after Curry?

96. Against which team did Curry make his 2000th career three-pointer?

97. Who was the head coach of the USA Men's National Basketball team when Curry played in the 2014 FIBA World Cup?

98. In 2020 which game show did Curry produce and star in?

99. In the 2019-2020 season how many games did Curry play largely due to injury?

100. Which Warriors teammate joined Curry as a "Splash Brother"?

101. Against which team did the Warriors complete a four-game sweep in the 2018 NBA Finals?

102. Who was the head coach of the USA Men's Basketball team during the 2016 Olympics which Curry opted out of?

103. Which NBA player famously blocked Curry's shot in Game 7 of the 2016 NBA Finals?

104. Who was the main point guard that Curry faced in the 2019 Western Conference Finals?

105. Which NBA player also from a small college did Curry say inspired him during his time at Davidson?

106. Which NBA player surpassed Curry's single-game three-pointer record by making 14 threes in a game?

107. Which documentary series that aired in 2018 was Curry an executive producer for?

108. What is the name of Stephen Curry's sister who played college volleyball?

109. How many threes did Curry make in the 2016 All-Star Game tying the All-Star Game record at the time?

110. Against which team did Curry set his then career-high of 54 points in 2013?

111. Against which team did Curry hit a game-winning three-pointer from nearly half-court in the 2015-2016 season?

112. Which legendary NBA player said Curry's shooting was changing the way the game was played?

113. Which NBA player from the 2009 draft class along with Curry became an MVP and NBA Champion?

114. In what year did Curry launch his "Underrated Tour" to help underrated high school athletes?

115. Which former NBA player and analyst claimed that Curry was "hurting the game" because young players tried to emulate his playing style?

116. What was the title of the YouTube series that Curry produced in 2018 focusing on his daily life?

117. What was the Warriors' regular-season record in Curry's second MVP season?

118. By the end of 2021 how many times had Curry been selected for the NBA All-Star game?

119. In the 2015-2016 season Curry made at least one three-pointer in how many consecutive games?

120. In which year did Curry launch his Underrated Tour a basketball camp for young players not highly ranked by the traditional system?

121. Who succeeded Mark Jackson as the head coach of the Golden State Warriors?

122. In 2021 Curry participated in an iteration of the NBA All-Star 3-point contest. Did he win?

123. In what year did Curry surpass Ray Allen for the most three-pointers made in a single postseason?

124. Against which team did Curry make his return from injury in the 2017 playoffs scoring 40 points?

125. How many points did Curry score in his first game back from injury in the 2018 playoffs?

126. In 2021 which team did Curry score 62 points against marking a career-high?

127. Which team did Curry face in his return game from injury during the 2019-2020 season?

128. Which NBA team did Stephen Curry's father Dell Curry end his career with?

129. What's the name of Curry's eldest daughter who gained fame for her post-game press conference appearances?

130. In which season did Curry first average more than 30 points per game?

131. Who was the main point guard that Curry and the Warriors defeated in the 2019 Western Conference Finals?

132. In the 2016 NBA Finals how many games were the Warriors ahead before the Cavaliers came back to win the title?

133. In 2012 Curry and which other Golden State player combined for an NBA record of 483 three-pointers in a single season?

134. How many regular-season MVPs does Curry's coach Steve Kerr have as a player?

135. Who was the starting center for the Warriors during Curry's first MVP season?

136. In what year did Stephen Curry release his first signature shoe with Under Armour?

137. In the 2015-2016 season how many games did the Warriors lose at home?

138. Which other NBA player from the same draft class as Curry became his teammate in the 2019-2020 season?

139. Against which team did the Warriors led by Curry come back from a 3-1 deficit in the 2016 Western Conference Finals?

140. How many points did Curry score in the 2011 NBA Skills Challenge during All-Star weekend?

141. In 2016 Curry set the record for most three-pointers made in a single game with 13. Against which team did he achieve this?

142. In which year did Curry surpass Ray Allen for the most career postseason three-pointers?

143. In which year did Curry and the Golden State Warriors set the record for the best start to a season winning their first 24 games?

144. How many three-pointers did Curry make in his record-setting 2012-2013 season?

145. Which musician mentioned Stephen Curry in the song "0 to 100/The Catch Up"?

146. Which award did Curry win during the 2010-2011 season highlighting his improvements from his rookie year?

147. Who was the first coach to name Curry as a starter in an NBA All-Star game?

148. Who was the Warriors' head coach during Stephen Curry's rookie season?

149. In which season did Curry first average more than 8 assists per game?

150. In which year did Curry and the Golden State Warriors not make the NBA playoffs after their successful run?

151. How many games did the Warriors win during Stephen Curry's rookie season?

152. Which former NBA player known for his three-point shooting said Curry and Thompson were the best shooting duo ever?

153. Which player was Curry's primary matchup in the 2019 Western Conference Finals?

154. Which other Davidson athlete was honored alongside Curry when his jersey was retired?

155. Which Children's Hospital did Curry support with a significant donation in 2019?

156. Who broke Curry's single-game three-point record by making 14 three-pointers in a game?

157. Which player was selected immediately after Stephen Curry in the 2009 NBA Draft?

158. In which year did Curry score a career-high 62 points in a regular-season game?

159. In the 2015-2016 season how many three-pointers did Curry make breaking his own record?

160. How many children do Stephen and Ayesha Curry have by the end of 2021?

161. In which year was Stephen Curry named the NBA Sportsmanship Award winner?

162. Which NBA legend known for his sky-hook shot praised Curry's ability to revolutionize the game?

163. Which former NBA MVP attended Davidson College decades before Curry and is known for mentoring him?

164. Who won the NBA MVP award in the year between Curry's two MVP seasons?

165. Which of Curry's three-point records was broken by James Harden in 2019?

166. What is the title of the documentary about Curry's journey during the 2018-2019 NBA season?

167. Which charity event did Curry participate in related to golfing in 2021?

168. Against which team did Curry suffer a major ankle injury in the 2011 playoffs?

169. Who was the starting point guard for the Golden State Warriors before Stephen Curry's arrival?

170. Who was Curry's teammate in 2013 known for his rebounding and shot-blocking abilities?

171. Which rapper mentioned Curry in the lyrics "Golden State running practice at my house"?

172. Which famous director made a comment about Curry being in his "next world" when he shoots?

173. Which former NBA player and coach has praised Curry for being the best shooter he's ever seen?

174. In 2020 Curry played in a golf event with which former NFL quarterback?

175. Who was the last player to lead the NBA in scoring before Curry achieved it in the 2015-2016 season?

176. In 2020 which Japanese player credited Curry as an inspiration for taking up basketball?

177. Against which team did Curry set the record for most points in an overtime period scoring 17 in 2016?

178. What is the maximum distance from which Curry has hit a three-pointer in an NBA game?

179. In which season did Curry break his own record by hitting 402 three-pointers?

180. Which two NBA players did Curry pick first for his team in the 2019 NBA All-Star game draft?

181. What's the name of Stephen Curry's younger brother also an NBA player?

182. In what year did the Warriors first reach the NBA playoffs with Curry on the roster?

183. In which city did Curry host a pop-up shop for his Under Armour shoes in 2017?

184. In which country did Stephen Curry play a series of exhibition games in the summer of 2011?

1. Portland Trail Blazers.

2. Kyrie Irving.

3. Orlando Magic.

4. 2.

5. 13.

6. 2.

7. Nike.

8. Klay Thompson.

9. 2010-2011.

10. 1st Round.

11. 2010-2011.

12. Charlotte North Carolina.

13. Chase Center.

14. Denver Nuggets.

15. Eat. Learn. Play.

16. Broken Left Hand.

17. Houston Rockets.

18. Under Armour.

19. LeBron James.

20. 2017.

21. Cleveland Cavaliers.

22. 1.

23. Kyle Lowry.

24. Golden State Warriors.

25. 157.

26. "Love Never Fails."

27. 2.1.

28. Seth Curry.

29. New Orleans Pelicans.

30. Ayesha Curry.

31. Portland Trail Blazers.

32. Sonya Curry.

33. Gregg Popovich.

34. Unanimous Media.

35. Kenny Smith.

36. 14.

37. Charles Barkley.

38. Andre Iguodala.

39. Cleveland Cavaliers.

40. James Harden.

41. Cleveland Cavaliers.

42. Mark Jackson.

43. Larry Riley.

44. Bob McKillop.

45. Chris Paul.

46. 6.

47. Shaun Livingston.

48. 30.

49. Bob Myers.

50. Barack Obama.

51. Cleveland Cavaliers.

52. Miami Heat.

53. Larry Riley.

54. 2.

55. Portland Trail Blazers.

56. Kevin Durant.

57. James Harden.

58. Monta Ellis.

59. Paul Pierce.

60. Hangzhou.

61. Three-point Shooting.

62. Canon W. Jack Curry.

63. 2015.

64. Best Male Athlete.

65. 26.

66. 3.

67. Ray Allen.

68. The Shimmy.

69. Tony Allen.

70. Ayesha Curry.

71. Memphis Grizzlies.

72. His Father Dell Curry.

73. Matthew Dellavedova.

74. Duke University.

75. Mark Jackson.

76. Los Angeles Clippers.

77. Klay Thompson.

78. 2015-2016.

79. Game 6.

80. 14.

81. "The Late Late Show With James Corden."

82. 3.

83. Eric Gordon.

84. Houston Rockets.

85. Shaquille O'Neal.

86. Dell Curry.

87. Ankle Injury.

88. 1.

89. Denver Nuggets.

90. Charlotte Christian School.

91. Dell Curry.

92. 2015-2016.

93. Steve Nash.

94. Houston Rockets.

95. Trae Young.

96. Memphis Grizzlies.

97. Mike Krzyzewski.

98. "Holey Moley".

99. 5.

100. Klay Thompson.

101. Cleveland Cavaliers.

102. Mike Krzyzewski.

103. LeBron James.

104. Damian Lillard.

105. Steve Nash.

106. Klay Thompson.

107. "Stephen Vs. The Game".

108. Sydel Curry.

109. 6.

110. New York Knicks.

111. Oklahoma City Thunder.

112. Magic Johnson.

113. James Harden.

114. 2019.

115. Charles Barkley.

116. "5 Minutes From Home."

117. 73-9.

118. 7.

119. 152.

120. 2019.

121. Steve Kerr.

122. Yes.

123. 2015.

124. Portland Trail Blazers.

125. 28.

126. Portland Trail Blazers.

127. Toronto Raptors.

128. Toronto Raptors.

129. Riley Curry.

130. 2015-2016.

131. Damian Lillard.

132. 3-1.

133. Klay Thompson.

134. 0.

135. Andrew Bogut.

136. 2015.

137. 2.

138. D'Angelo Russell.

139. Oklahoma City Thunder.

140. 28.

141. New Orleans Pelicans.

142. 2019.

143. 2015.

144. 272.

145. Drake.

146. NBA's Most Improved Player.

147. Steve Kerr.

148. Don Nelson.

149. 2013-2014.

150. 2020.

151. 26.

152. Reggie Miller.

153. Damian Lillard.

154. Emily Wampler.

155. Oakland's Children's Hospital.

156. Klay Thompson.

157. Jordan Hill.

158. 2021.

159. 402.

160. 3.

161. 2011.

162. Kareem Abdul-Jabbar.

163. Charles Barkley.

164. James Harden.

165. Most Threes Made In A Month.

166. "Stephen Vs. The Game".

167. The Match.

168. Denver Nuggets.

169. Monta Ellis.

170. Andrew Bogut.

171. Drake.

172. Spike Lee.

173. Steve Kerr.

174. Peyton Manning.

175. Kevin Durant.

176. Rui Hachimura.

177. Portland Trail Blazers.

178. About 62 Feet.

179. 2015-2016.

180. Giannis Antetokounmpo And Joel Embiid.

181. Seth Curry.

182. 2013.

183. Oakland.

184. Taiwan.

1. Curry surpassed which player in 2015 for most three-pointers made in a single postseason?

2. How many assists did Curry average during his unanimous MVP season?

3. In which season did Curry first average more than 8 assists per game?

4. What is the full name of Steph Curry's wife?

5. Which childhood friend of Curry's also played in the NBA and even teamed up with him on the Warriors?

6. Against which team did Curry record his first NBA triple-double?

7. In the 2015 NBA Finals Curry set a record for most three-pointers made in a Finals series. How many did he make?

8. How many points did Curry average in his unanimous MVP season?

9. In 2016 Curry surpassed which former NBA player for most three-pointers made in a single month?

10. As of 2021 how many children does Stephen Curry have?

11. In 2018 Stephen Curry and which other NBA player led a venture to bring the Carolina Panthers of the NFL under new ownership?

12. Which team drafted Stephen Curry's younger brother Seth?

13. Against which team did Curry achieve his highest-scoring playoff game as of 2021?

14. Against which team did Curry make his NBA debut?

15. Against which team did Curry suffer a notable injury in the 2016 playoffs causing him to miss several games?

16. What is the name of Stephen Curry's son?

17. In the 2018 Western Conference Finals the Warriors faced and defeated which team to advance to the Finals?

18. Curry often shouts which phrase after making a big shot?

19. Curry played alongside which other guard in the 2014 FIBA Basketball World Cup?

20. Who served as Curry's backup during his unanimous MVP season?

21. Which NBA team did Curry's father Dell Curry spend the majority of his career playing for?

22. What unusual game-day routine does Curry have involving candy?

23. Which team did Curry's Warriors face in the 2018 Western Conference Semifinals?

24. Who was Curry's coach at Davidson College?

25. Against which team did Curry score a then career-high 54 points in Madison Square Garden during the 2012-2013 season?

26. How many points did Curry score in his NBA debut?

27. Which team did Curry's Warriors face in the first round of the 2016 playoffs?

28. How many three-pointers did Curry make in his rookie season?

29. In which season did Curry surpass 200 three-pointers for the first time in his career?

30. How many games did Curry's Warriors win in the 2018 NBA Playoffs?

31. Who served as the interim head coach for the Warriors in the early part of the 2015-2016 season due to Steve Kerr's health issues?

32. How many games did the Warriors win during Curry's rookie season?

33. Curry's brother Seth has played for the NBA's Dallas Mavericks and which other NBA team as of 2021?

34. In what round and at what overall pick was Curry drafted?

35. Who was the Warriors' leading scorer in the season before Curry's arrival?

36. In which year did Curry's Under Armour shoe line officially launch?

37. Who was the head coach of the Golden State Warriors before Steve Kerr took over?

38. In which season did Curry win the ESPY award for Best Male Athlete?

39. Curry has made how many All-NBA First Team appearances as of the end of the 2021 season?

40. Which two players were drafted ahead of Curry in the 2009 NBA Draft?

41. What distinction did Curry achieve in the 2012-2013 season related to three-pointers?

42. In which NBA Draft was Curry selected?

43. Which team did the Warriors face in the 2019 Western Conference Finals?

44. What is the middle name of Stephen Curry?

45. How many free throws did Curry make consecutively to set an NBA record in 2019?

46. In his unanimous MVP season how many games did Curry's Warriors win?

47. Which former NBA point guard did Curry pass in 2019 to move into 3rd place for most three-pointers made in a career?

48. How many MVP awards did Curry win before the age of 30?

49. What was the first model name of Curry's signature shoe line with Under Armour?

50. Against which team did Curry achieve his career-high scoring game?

51. Against which team did Curry famously turn around before his three-pointer went in during a game in the 2015-2016 season?

52. Curry made his NBA playoff debut in which year?

53. How many points did Curry average during his senior year at Davidson?

54. Who is the eldest Curry sibling?

55. Which team did Curry and the Warriors face in the 2019 Western Conference Finals?

56. Against which team did Curry have his first career triple-double?

57. Who was the coach of the U.S. National Team when Curry won the gold medal in the 2014 World Cup?

58. How many three-pointers did Curry make in his rookie season?

59. In 2013 which former NBA player said he thought Curry and Klay Thompson were the best shooting backcourt duo in NBA history?

60. Who was Curry's head coach in his rookie season?

61. Which former NBA MVP known for his time with the Boston Celtics mentioned that he believes Curry might be the best point guard of all time?

62. Which shoe company does Stephen Curry have an endorsement deal with?

63. Which former NBA player and ESPN analyst has often been critical of Curry suggesting he's not a top player?

64. Curry made his NBA All-Star Game debut in which season?

65. Which Western Conference team did Curry's Warriors defeat in the 2015 NBA Finals to win the championship?

66. What is the name of Curry's oldest daughter?

67. In the 2015-2016 season how many consecutive home games did the Warriors win setting an NBA record?

68. In which year did Stephen Curry first lead the NBA in jersey sales?

69. In the 2019 NBA Finals who was the primary defender for the Toronto Raptors tasked with guarding Curry?

70. Which team drafted Curry's father Dell Curry?

71. How many three-point contests during the NBA All-Star Weekend has Curry won as of 2021?

72. Curry's sister Sydel played which sport at Elon University?

73. Curry and which other player are the only two in NBA history to make 300 three-pointers in a single season?

74. Which high school did Stephen Curry attend?

75. Curry's brother Seth played for which team during the 2019 Western Conference Finals?

76. In which season did Curry first average over 30 points per game?

77. How many seasons did it take Curry to score his 14 000th point in the NBA?

78. How many points did Curry score in his first-ever NBA playoff game?

79. Which Hollywood actor played a one-on-one game with Curry for a charity event in 2017?

80. Which NBA team did Curry face in his first-ever NBA playoff series?

81. How many rebounds per game did Curry average during the 2015-2016 season?

82. How many points did Curry score in his NBA debut?

83. Which musical artist wrote a song named "Steph Curry" that released in 2019?

84. Against which team did Curry score his 10 000th career point?

85. Which famous actor did Curry play golf with in a 2019 episode of "Holey Moley"?

86. Who held the Warriors' record for most three-pointers before Curry?

87. Which legendary player once claimed Curry was "hurting the game" because young players tried to emulate his deep three-point shots?

88. Stephen Curry once scored 54 points in a legendary performance at which iconic basketball arena?

89. In the 2016-2017 season Curry set a personal and NBA record for how many three-pointers in a single game?

90. Which team did the Warriors defeat to achieve a record-breaking 73rd win in the 2015-2016 regular season?

91. Who did the Warriors defeat in the Western Conference Finals en route to their 2015 NBA championship?

92. Which NBA player known for his fierce defense claimed in an interview that he loves "the challenge of trying to guard" Curry?

93. Which Hall of Famer once said that Curry was "just a shooter" and couldn't handle the ball?

94. Which point guard was the only one selected before Curry in the 2009 NBA Draft?

95. In the 2017-2018 season Curry made 5 or more three-pointers in how many consecutive games?

96. In which city was the 2019 NBA All-Star Game held where Curry participated?

97. In which year did Curry first represent the USA in a major international basketball competition?

98. In 2013 Curry and which other player set the NBA record for most combined three-pointers by a pair of teammates in a single season?

99. What special distinction did Curry achieve in the 2016 NBA All-Star Game?

100. How many seasons had Curry played in the NBA as of the end of the 2020 season?

101. In a comedic video segment for which television network did Curry "teach" viewers how to do the perfect three-point celebration?

102. In a commercial for which brand did Curry famously "make it rain" with a broken sprinkler?

103. Against which Western Conference team did Curry score 40 points in his return from a 10-game injury absence in the 2018-2019 season?

104. In the 2018 playoffs Curry set a record for three-pointers in a single postseason. How many did he make?

105. In 2016 Curry set an NBA record by making a three-pointer in how many consecutive regular-season games?

106. Who was Curry's teammate at Davidson who also had a brief NBA career?

107. Curry was named the NBA Western Conference Player of the Week how many times during the 2014-2015 season?

108. In 2017 Curry participated in a professional golf tournament on which tour?

109. Which renowned coach described Curry as "transformative" due to his shooting ability and influence on the game?

110. Which former player known for his iconic skyhook shot praised Curry's ability to score without dunking?

111. In a touching moment during a game Curry once swapped shoes with a boy suffering from which disease?

112. Who was the primary defender from the Cleveland Cavaliers that often matched up against Curry in the NBA Finals?

113. Which charity is notably supported by Stephen Curry to combat malaria?

114. In which season did Curry become the Warriors' all-time leader in three-pointers made?

115. Whatâ€™s the name of Stephen Curry's younger brother who also plays in the NBA?

116. Which NBA legend known for his skyhook praised Curry for his creative genius on the court?

117. Against which team did Curry sink a long-range three-pointer in overtime shouting "I'm back!" after a notable injury absence?

118. Which current NBA player and brother of Stephen Curry also plays in the league as of 2021?

119. Which NBA player did Curry face off against in a 2015 Under Armour commercial?

120. In which season did Curry first average more than 30 points per game?

121. Against which team did Curry debut his Under Armour Curry 4 shoes in the 2017 NBA Finals?

122. Who was the previous record-holder for most three-pointers in a single season before Curry broke it?

123. Curry is known for a pre-game ritual that involves which sport other than basketball?

124. What number did Curry wear during his college basketball career at Davidson?

125. What distinction did Curry achieve in 2015 joining Mark Price as the only other player to do so?

126. Which Eastern Conference team did Curry score a career-high 54 points against in 2013?

127. Curry once made a guest appearance on which famous cooking show featuring his wife as a host?

128. In 2019 how many games did Curry play before suffering a broken hand injury?

129. How many points did Curry average in the NBA Finals series where the Warriors were defeated by the Toronto Raptors in 2019?

130. Which team did Curry score 17 points against in overtime an NBA record for points in OT?

131. Which team did the Warriors defeat in the 2017 NBA Finals to win their second title in three years?

132. Who was Curry's main backup at point guard in the 2017 NBA championship season?

133. Curry achieved a triple-double in the 2017 NBA Finals against which team?

134. During the 2013 NBA playoffs Curry set a record for the most three-pointers in a single postseason with how many?

135. Which NBA team did Curry play against in his first Christmas Day game?

136. In the 2016 NBA Finals Golden State held a 3-1 lead. Which team came back to win the championship that year?

137. Which former NBA point guard famous for his time with the Utah Jazz did Curry surpass on the all-time three-pointers made list?

138. What accolade did Curry win in the 2011 NBA Skills Challenge during All-Star Weekend?

139. Against which team did Curry record a double-double in his first NBA playoff game?

140. Who was the Golden State Warriors' general manager when Curry was drafted?

141. How many games did the Warriors lose at home during their record-setting 73-win season?

142. In 2015 Stephen Curry appeared on which popular late-night talk show where he played a game of one-on-one with the host?

143. Which former NBA point guard known for his flashy assists claimed that Curry is "changing the game" in a positive way?

144. Against which team did Curry hit a game-winner in the 2019 playoffs helping the Warriors advance to the next round?

145. Against which team did Curry famously drop 53 points on his 28th birthday?

146. Which NBA player has the nickname "The Greek Freak" and has had memorable matchups against Curry?

147. In 2018 who surpassed Curry for the record of most three-pointers in a single postseason?

148. Curry's daughter Riley famously stole the show during which year's NBA playoff post-game press conferences?

149. Curry was named Western Conference Player of the Month how many times during the 2015-2016 season?

150. In the early part of his career Curry had chronic issues with which part of his body?

151. Which NBA player also from Davidson was known as a mentor to Curry during his early NBA years?

152. Who did Curry beat in the final round of the 2021 NBA Three-Point Contest?

153. Against which NBA team did Curry have this 54-point performance at Madison Square Garden?

154. Which NBA legend commented in 2016 that his own team from the 90s would've "killed" Curry's Warriors?

155. Against which team did Curry have a playoff career-high 47 points in the 2019 NBA Finals?

156. Which legendary NBA team did the 2015-2016 Warriors surpass to achieve their record 73-win season?

157. Which NBA team did the Warriors beat in 2019 to advance to their fifth consecutive NBA Finals?

158. Curry's Warriors faced and defeated which team in the first round of the 2015 NBA Playoffs?

159. What distinct colorway did Under Armour release in 2016 that became a subject of internet jokes?

160. In 2016 which team eliminated the Warriors in the Western Conference playoffs breaking their quest for a three-peat?

161. In 2020 Steph Curry was out for the majority of the season due to an injury to which part of his body?

162. In 2017 Curry avoided suspension for throwing his mouthguard in a game against which team?

163. Which former NBA star claimed Curry was "hurting the game" because young players were trying to emulate his style?

164. Curry is known to wear which jersey number throughout his NBA career?

165. Which NBA player known for his defensive prowess said in 2017 that Curry "doesn't get enough credit" for his defense?

166. How many steals per game did Curry average during the 2015-2016 season when he was named MVP?

167. Who did Curry beat in the finals of the 2015 NBA Three-Point Contest?

168. Which team did the Warriors beat in 2015 to advance to the NBA Finals for the first time in 40 years?

169. What nickname is given to the duo of Stephen Curry and Klay Thompson?

170. How many games did Curry's Warriors win during the 2014-2015 regular season?

171. Curry achieved how many points during his career-high game as of 2021?

172. Against which team did Curry have a game where he made 11 three-pointers and scored 51 points in 2018?

173. In which year did Stephen Curry surpass Ray Allen's career total of playoff three-pointers?

174. Which legendary coach called Stephen Curry "a transformational player" due to his impact on the modern NBA?

175. In the 2015-2016 season the Warriors began with a winning streak. How many games did they win consecutively?

176. How many turnovers did Curry average during his unanimous MVP season?

177. Which award did Stephen Curry win in the 2011 NBA All-Star festivities?

178. Which team did Curry make his return against in the 2020 season after a long injury hiatus?

179. Who did the Warriors defeat in the 2015 NBA Finals to win their first championship with Curry?

1. Reggie Miller.

2. 6.7.

3. 2013-2014.

4. Ayesha Curry.

5. Kent Bazemore.

6. Los Angeles Clippers.

7. 27.

8. 30.1 Points.

9. George McCloud.

10. 3.

11. Diddy (Sean Combs).

12. Sacramento Kings.

13. Portland Trail Blazers.

14. Houston Rockets.

15. Houston Rockets.

16. Canon Curry.

17. Houston Rockets.

18. "I'm Here!"

19. Kyrie Irving.

20. Shaun Livingston.

21. Charlotte Hornets.

22. He Eats Popcorn Before Games.

23. New Orleans Pelicans.

24. Bob McKillop.

25. New York Knicks.

26. 14.

27. Houston Rockets.

28. 166.

29. 2012-2013.

30. 16.

31. Luke Walton.

32. 26.

33. Philadelphia 76ers.

34. 1st Round 7th Overall.

35. Monta Ellis.

36. 2015.

37. Mark Jackson.

38. 2015.

39. 3 Times.

40. Blake Griffin And Hasheem Thabeet.

41. Broke The Record For Most Three-pointers In A Single Season.

42. 2009.

43. Portland Trail Blazers.

44. Wardell.

45. 97.

46. 73.

47. Kyle Korver.

48. 2.

49. Curry One.

50. Portland Trail Blazers.

51. Memphis Grizzlies.

52. 2013.

53. 28.6.

54. Sydel Curry.

55. Portland Trail Blazers.

56. Los Angeles Clippers.

57. Mike Krzyzewski.

58. 166.

59. Reggie Miller.

60. Don Nelson.

61. Magic Johnson.

62. Under Armour.

63. Paul Pierce.

64. 2013-2014.

65. Cleveland Cavaliers.

66. Riley Curry.

67. 54.

68. 2015.

69. Fred VanVleet.

70. Utah Jazz.

71. 2.

72. Volleyball.

73. James Harden.

74. Charlotte Christian School.

75. Portland Trail Blazers.

76. 2015-2016.

77. 10 Seasons.

78. 19.

79. Joel McHale.

80. Denver Nuggets.

81. 5.4.

82. 14 Points.

83. Drake.

84. Memphis Grizzlies.

85. Bill Murray.

86. Chris Mullin.

87. Charles Barkley.

88. Madison Square Garden.

89. 13.

90. Memphis Grizzlies.

91. Houston Rockets.

92. Patrick Beverley.

93. Isiah Thomas.

94. Ricky Rubio.

95. 7.

96. Charlotte.

97. 2010.

98. Klay Thompson.

99. He Was The Top Vote-getter.

100. 11 Seasons.

101. ESPN.

102. State Farm.

103. Memphis Grizzlies.

104. 98.

105. 157.

106. Jermareo Davidson.

107. 4 Times.

108. Web.com Tour.

109. Gregg Popovich.

110. Kareem Abdul-Jabbar.

111. Leukemia.

112. Kyrie Irving.

113. Nothing But Nets.

114. 2012-2013.

115. Seth Curry.

116. Kareem Abdul-Jabbar.

117. Portland Trail Blazers.

118. Seth Curry.

119. Jamie Foxx.

120. 2015-2016.

121. Cleveland Cavaliers.

122. Ray Allen.

123. Volleyball.

124. 30.

125. Shooting 50/40/90 While Averaging 20+ Points.

126. New York Knicks.

127. "Ayesha's Home Kitchen".

128. 4 Games.

129. 30.5.

130. Portland Trail Blazers.

131. Cleveland Cavaliers.

132. Shaun Livingston.

133. Cleveland Cavaliers.

134. 98.

135. Cleveland Cavaliers.

136. Cleveland Cavaliers.

137. John Stockton.

138. Champion.

139. Denver Nuggets.

140. Larry Riley.

141. 2.

142. "The Late Show With Stephen Colbert".

143. Steve Nash.

144. Houston Rockets.

145. New Orleans Pelicans.

146. Giannis Antetokounmpo.

147. Klay Thompson.

148. 2015.

149. 3 Times.

150. Ankles.

151. Jason Richardson.

152. Mike Conley.

153. New York Knicks.

154. Oscar Robertson.

155. Toronto Raptors.

156. 1995-1996 Chicago Bulls.

157. Portland Trail Blazers.

158. New Orleans Pelicans.

159. "Chef Curry".

160. Toronto Raptors.

161. Hand.

162. Memphis Grizzlies.

163. Charles Barkley.

164. 30.

165. Kawhi Leonard.

166. 2.1.

167. Klay Thompson.

168. Houston Rockets.

169. Splash Brothers.

170. 67 Games.

171. 62.

172. Washington Wizards.

173. 2019.

174. Phil Jackson.

175. 24.

176. 3.3.

177. Skills Challenge.

178. Toronto Raptors.

179. Cleveland Cavaliers.